Idaho
impressions

photography by
Leland Howard

FARCOUNTRY
PRESS

Front cover: McGown Peak, Sawtooth Wilderness Area.

Back cover: Arrowleaf balsamroot, Cache National Forest.

Title page: Arrowleaf balsamroot on a ridge in Caribou National Forest.

Right: Pack River in 904,081-acre Kaniksu National Forest. The Pack River's headwaters lie in the Selkirk Range, and it drains into Lake Pend Oreille.

Below: The syringa, Idaho state flower since 1931. PHOTO BY WILLIAM H. MULLINS

ISBN 10: 1-56037-297-4
ISBN 13: 978-1-56037-297-4
Photography © 2004 Leland Howard
© 2004 Farcountry Press

For more information on our books write Farcountry Press, P.O. Box 5630, Helena, MT 59604; call (800) 821-3874; or visit www.farcountrypress.com

Created, produced, and designed in the United States. Printed in China.
12 11 10 09 08   2 3 4 5

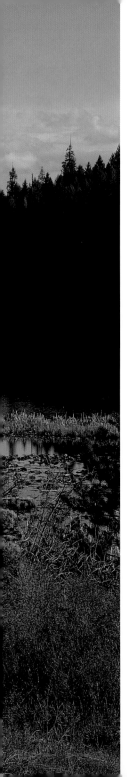

Left: Remnants of an old cabin near a high mountain lake in the Purcell Mountains.

Below: Copper Creek Falls, Kaniksu National Forest. This 80-foot waterfall is accessed by a good hiking trail through a beautiful forested landscape.

Right: Bull elk crossing the Selway River, Selway-Bitterroot Wilderness Area.

Below: American Falls, Upper Priest Scenic Area. The Upper Priest River winds its way through old-growth forests of western red cedar and western white pine (the state tree) in Kaniksu National Forest.

Above: Lower Mesa Falls, located in the Targhee National Forest portion of the Greater Yellowstone Ecosystem, drops 65 feet to the gorge below.

Left: The mirrorlike waters of the St. Joe River in spring. In 1978, 66.3 miles of the river from the North Fork to St. Joe Lake were designated part of the National Wild and Scenic Rivers System.

Right: Aspens in fall finery, Sawtooth Valley south of Stanley. The stretch of Idaho Highway 75 that runs north of Ketchum over Galena Summit and into Stanley offers unequaled views—especially during the height of fall color.

Below: Whitewater rafting on the Snake River. Often described as "the whitewater state," Idaho offers many world-class whitewater runs.

Above: The South Fork of the Snake River and Fall Creek Falls in winter's icy grip.

Right: Heavy snow falls from the drooping branches of conifers in Harriman State Park, a 10,000-acre park given to the citizens of Idaho by the Harriman family in 1977; the area is a favorite for cross-country skiing.

Far right: Falls River meanders through frozen terrain. This river originates in Yellowstone National Park and flows west into Idaho before merging with the Henrys Fork of the Snake River.

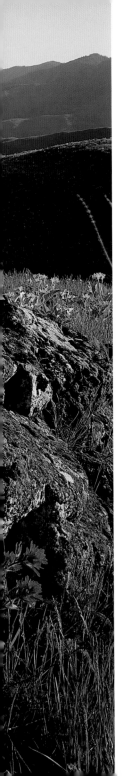

Above: Mountain bluebird, Idaho's state bird. PHOTO BY WILLIAM H. MULLINS

Left: Desert paintbrush and arrowleaf balsamroot color the slopes of Hells Canyon. Reaching 9,300 feet in depth in some areas, Hells Canyon is considered the deepest river gorge in North America.

Right: Alpine shooting stars seem to create a lake of red in the 756,000-acre Sawtooth Recreation Area, established by U.S. Congress in 1972.

Below: Huckleberry bushes bring vivid color to Boise National Forest in autumn.

Night skiing at Bogus Basin Ski
Area, with Boise in the distance.
PHOTO BY STEVE BLY

Facing page: The Northern Pacific Depot Railroad Museum in Wallace is listed on the National Register of Historic Places. This chateau-style depot was constructed at the turn of the century with brick imported from China and concrete panels made from mine tailings.

Below: The Oasis Bordello Museum in Wallace first served as a hotel and saloon in 1895. It is one of the few structures in Wallace to survive the famous 1910 fire.

Above: Autumn graces the Boulder Mountains north of Ketchum.

Left: The South Fork of the Snake River stretches more than 60 miles from Palisades Dam to its confluence with the Henry's Fork.

Stanley Lake, in the Sawtooth Wilderness Area, rests in a glacier-carved valley about 5 miles north of Stanley.

Right: Stunning sunrise at High Up Lake in the Beaverhead Mountains of the Bitterroot Range.

Below: Day's end at Lake Pend Oreille, the largest lake in Idaho. The lake's length is 65 miles and its greatest width is 15 miles; its depth is thought to be in excess of 1,170 feet.

Left: Arrowleaf balsamroot and desert paintbrush in Cache National Forest.

Below: Delicate tiger lily in the inland rainforest of Kaniksu National Forest. This species of lily is becoming increasingly difficult to find in the wild as habitat diminishes.

Above: Bear grass on a ridge in Coeur d'Alene National Forest seems to glow at sunrise.

Right: Daybreak reflected in a pond in Targhee National Forest near Island Park.

Above: Waterfall near appropriately named Waterfall Trail in the Craig Mountains, Frank Church–River of No Return Wilderness Area. The Bighorn Crags in the background form a high granite divide 20 miles long and up to 10 miles wide; they rise nearly 1,000 feet above the surrounding mountains.

Left: Howard Lake in the Pioneer Mountains, a spectacular range with many peaks

Right: Camas, yellow pea, and Rydberg's penstemon flourish in Musselshell Meadows, Nez Perce National Historic Site in Clearwater National Forest.

Below: The town of Clark Fork was established when the Northern Pacific Railroad built its main line through northern Idaho in the 1880s.

Above: Early nineteenth century pioneer cabin, Lemhi Mountains.

Right: American badger peering out from its den, Little Lost Valley.

Far right: An old barn withstands weather and time near the 13,000-foot spires of the Teton Mountains. Now called Teton Valley, fur trappers called this area Pierre's Hole.

Above: Cowboy kitchen—a common setup used by wilderness guides and outfitters.

Facing page: Bull moose wandering the woodlands of Targhee National Forest.

Right: Fall Creek Falls tumbles into the South Fork of the Snake River amid autumn hues.

Facing page: The Owyhee River slicing through the canyon at sunset.

Above: Lightning flashes over the Snake River Plain.

Left: Winter sunrise at City of Rocks National Reserve. Some of the granite rock formations here are thought to be several billion years old. They are some of the oldest formations found in the continental United States.

Above: Pass Creek cuts a path through the pristine forests of the Lost River Range.

Right: Eldorado Creek along the Lewis and Clark National Historic Trail, Clearwater National Forest. It is believed that this is the spot referred to as "Small Prairie Camp" in the Lewis and Clark Journals.

Above: These granite formations along the Goodales Cutoff section of the Oregon Trail were used as landmarks by pioneers in wagon trains.

Left: A brilliant sunset paints pink the South Fork of the Snake River and the Church of Jesus Christ of Latter-day Saints Temple in Idaho Falls.

Above: Female chipping sparrow and chicks in the Lost River Range. The forest edges and clearings in this semi-arid range provide good habitat for this species.

Right: Caribou Mountain rises above hills gilded by autumn's touch.

Left: The scenic Selway River reflects the pristine forest that fringes its banks, Selway-Bitterroot Wilderness Area.

Below: Lower Mesa Falls in autumn.

Right: A winter wonderland in Harriman State Park.

Below: Cross-country ski tracks in the Snake River Mountains.

Above: The Eastern Idaho State Fair in Blackfoot is an annual event that features big-name musicians and draws visitors from across the nation.

Left: Little Lost Valley aglow with the last fiery moments of daylight.

Right: Statue of Sacajawea and infant Jean Baptiste at the Sacajawea Interpretive, Cultural, and Education Center in Salmon.
PHOTO BY WILLIAM H. MULLINS

Far right: Stately 11,815-foot Castle Peak in the White Cloud Mountains.

Above: A peaceful morning is reflected in a pond in the Prairie Centennial Marsh Wildlife Management Area, a 3,100-acre sanctuary for waterfowl and other wildlife.

Left: Field awash in the pastels of the common camas, Prairie Centennial Marsh Wildlife Management Area.

Right: Chukar partridge, an introduced species native to the Middle East, surveying its surroundings in the Owyhee Desert.

Far right: The breathtaking Lochsa River, Clearwater National Forest. Named for the Nez Perce word for "rough water," the Lochsa is paralleled by an Indian trading and hunting route that was followed by the Lewis and Clark Expedition.

Below: Herd of pronghorn antelope ambling up a hillside in Craters of the Moon National Monument and Preserve. A link to the Ice Age, pronghorns are an ancient species dating back 20 million years.

Above: Red-shafted flicker perched at its nesting hole, Pioneer Mountains.

Left: Day's end at Goat Lake, Sawtooth Wilderness Area. There are more than 140 high mountain lakes in the Sawtooth Wilderness Area.

Right: Path winding through shady old-growth forest in Kaniksu National Forest.

Far right: The Kootenai River, the headwaters of which are in southeastern British Columbia's Kootenay National Park, is the second-largest tributary to the Columbia River system in terms of runoff volume; it is the third largest in terms of drainage area. Only the Snake River contributes more volume—and does so from a much larger watershed area.

Above: Gathering wildflowers and making memories in the Lemhi Mountains.

Left: The Deadwood River reflects a vivid sky, Boise National Forest.

Above: Granite formations in City of Rocks National Reserve. Millions of years of erosion have carved extraordinary forms in this hard stone, which is some of the oldest exposed rock on earth.

Facing page: The Old Mission (formerly Mission of the Sacred Heart) is the oldest standing building in Idaho. Built between 1848 and 1853 by Jesuit missionaries and Coeur d'Alene Indians, it is an impressive hand-built structure held together by wooden pegs, straw, and river mud.

Right: Canola field in "the Palouse," a 4,000-square-mile area in Idaho and Washington known for its excellent farming conditions.

Below: Columbines, these in the Frank Church–River of No Return Wilderness, are found in moist woods, along streams, and on sunny talus slopes.

Above: The St. Joe River, swollen with spring runoff.

Facing page: Hiker resting amid Lewis's monkeyflowers near Homer Peak, which is reflected in Little Lake, Beaverhead Mountains, Bitterroot Range. This species is named in honor of Meriwether Lewis of the Lewis and Clark Expedition. Lewis first collected specimens of this plant in 1805 near Lemhi Pass in Montana.

Left: Wildhorse Lake outlet stream in the Pioneer Mountains.

Facing page: The Centennial Mountains sparkle with the day's last light.

Right: Calf roping at the Dodge National Circuit Finals Rodeo in Pocatello.

Below: The art of a bronc riders grip, Dodge National Circuit Finals Rodeo.

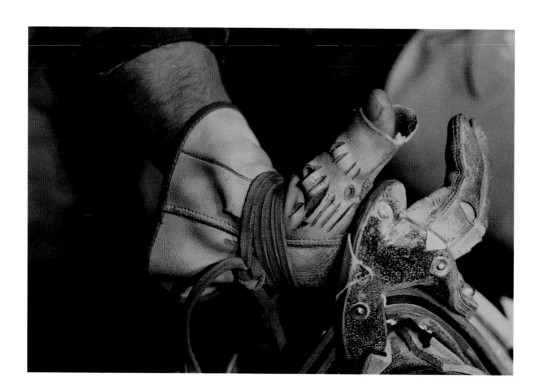

Above: Folks gathering for the Fourth of July fireworks display in Idaho Falls.

Left: Watching a dramatic sunset, Coeur d'Alene Lake.

*F*or a true artist, the tools of the trade become an extension of the self. For photographers, this is especially true. Anyone can pick up a camera, but mastery of that ineffable "eye" that marks a body of work as uniquely individual takes time. Leland Howard has devoted more than twenty years to his art as a nature photographer. Though the mechanics of photography are now second nature to him, seeing the image he wants to capture is a process that transcends words and is, in a sense, new every time. This freshness of approach is evident in the range of moods his photos evoke, and in the evolving sensibility of this Idaho artist.

Leland Howard has an exceptionally detailed knowledge of the rough-and-tumble territory of America's "wild west." Areas that can only be accessed by hiking, backpacking, and cross-country skiing are part of the challenge and part of the reward. The patience to wait out a storm, the diligence it takes to explore access routes that aren't on the map—these traits are just part of the toolbox for Howard. He takes them for granted, we revel in the results.

Howard's many credits include diverse publications by the National Geographic Society, Hallmark, AT&T, Sierra Press, Browntrout, Audubon, Healthy Planet, *PhotoGraphic*, Beautiful America Publications, Angel Graphics, Portal Publications, *Outside,* Blue Sky Publishing, Reiman Publications, Smith Western, Sierra Club, Great Mountain West, Western Image, Westcliffe Publishers, Northwest Publications and hundreds more.

www.LelandHoward.com